'Whether you are just starting to explore the Christian faith, or have been a follower of Jesus for years, here is an essential guide for the journey. Drawing deeply on Scripture and on inspiring stories of fellow travellers, Rowan Williams writes with a gentle strength that witnesses to the joy to be found in being disciples of Jesus.'

Kate Bottley, '*Gogglebox* vicar', writer, broadcaster and parish priest

'If discipleship is a journey, this short book belongs in the rucksack. With disarming simplicity, Rowan Williams invites us to a way of life that is profoundly attentive, generously forgiving and always drawn to service and joy. Like the Scriptures on which it is based, this book deserves repeated reading.'

Stephen Cherry, Dean of King's College, Cambridge

'Rowan Williams digs six deep wells into Scripture and the Christian tradition on the essentials of the Christian life. This short and profound book will help many Christians to explore more of what it means to be a disciple and to grow in relationship, in fruitfulness, in service and in joy'.

Steven Croft, Bishop of Oxford

'Rowan Williams is one of the great theologians of our time. He is also an inspiring teacher whose godly wisdom helps us to understand profound truths.'

Nicky Gumbel, Vicar of Holy Trinity Brompton and pioneer of the Alpha Course

'In this gentle and challenging book, Rowan Williams gives us both a clear explanation of what discipleship is and a stirring vision of what our discipleship can do. It is a beautifully crafted book that gives the reader real food for thought and sustenance for the journey . . . Each chapter would make for wonderful house-group discussion material.'

Jude Levermore, Head of Discipleship and
Ministries, The Methodist Church

'A wonderful book, and a treat in store for any reader. Dr Williams possesses an inarguably fine mind but also writes with the pen of a poet. It perfectly encapsulates the well-worn phrase "simplicity on the other side of complexity", which makes it accessible as well as heart-warming. This gem of a book is clearly born of his own deep love for, and closeness to, Jesus.'

Eleanor Mumford, founder of Vineyard
Churches, UK and Ireland

'Here is quite the most beautiful writing on discipleship I know. I am grateful for the inspiration that I find in these pages. I commend it to those who have been on this journey a long time, as well as to anyone who wonders what on earth following Jesus is all about.'

Justin Welby, Archbishop of Canterbury

Born in 1950, Rowan Williams was educated in Swansea (Wales) and Cambridge. He studied for his theology doctorate in Oxford, after which he taught theology in a seminary near Leeds. From 1977 until 1986, he was engaged in academic and parish work in Cambridge, before returning to Oxford as Lady Margaret Professor of Divinity. In 1990 he became a fellow of the British Academy.

In 1992 Professor Williams became Bishop of Monmouth, and in 1999 he was elected as Archbishop of Wales. He became Archbishop of Canterbury in late 2002 with ten years' experience as a diocesan bishop and three as a primate in the Anglican Communion. As archbishop, his main responsibilities were pastoral – whether leading his own diocese of Canterbury and the Church of England, or guiding the Anglican Communion worldwide. At the end of 2012, after ten years as archbishop, he stepped down and moved to a new role as Master of Magdalene College, Cambridge.

Professor Williams is acknowledged internationally as an outstanding theological writer and teacher as well as an accomplished poet and translator. His interests include music, fiction and languages.

BEING DISCIPLES

Essentials of the Christian life

Rowan Williams

First published in Great Britain in 2016

Society for Promoting Christian Knowledge
36 Causton Street
London SW1P 4ST
www.spck.org.uk

British Library Cataloguing-in-Publication Data
A catalogue record for this book is available from the British Library

ISBN 978–0–281–07662–8
eBook ISBN 978–0–281–07663–5

Typeset by Graphicraft Limited, Hong Kong
First printed in Great Britain by Ashford Colour Press
Subsequently digitally printed in Great Britain

eBook by Graphicraft Limited, Hong Kong

Produced on paper from sustainable forests

Contents

Acknowledgements

The chapters in this book are based on addresses originally given between 2007 and 2012, as follows:

Being disciples

27 April 2007, Fulcrum Conference
<http://rowanwilliams.archbishopofcanterbury.org/articles.php/2113/being-disciples-2007-fulcrum-conference-address#sthash.aZcv7Noe.dpuf>

Faith, hope and charity in tomorrow's world

6 March 2010, Lincoln Cathedral
<http://rowanwilliams.archbishopofcanterbury.org/articles.php/584/faith-hope-and-charity-in-tomorrows-world#sthash.UsHWstfL.dpuf>

Give us this day our daily bread

22 July 2010, Lutheran World Federation Assembly
<http://rowanwilliams.archbishopofcanterbury.org/articles.php/572/give-us-this-day-our-daily-bread-archbishops-address-at-lutheran-world-federation-assembly#sthash.D2vRJUhT.dpuf>

The meaning of holiness

4 November 2012, Diocese of Christchurch
<http://rowanwilliams.archbishopofcanterbury.org/articles.

php/2689/archbishop-reflects-on-holiness-with-young-adults-in-christchurch#sthash.c8T1dDfO.dpuf>

Public religion and the common good

12 May 2007, St Andrew's Cathedral, Singapore
<http://rowanwilliams.archbishopofcanterbury.org/articles.php/1165/christianity-public-religion-and-the-common-good>

Staying spiritually healthy

26 May 2012, Diocese of Coventry
<http://rowanwilliams.archbishopofcanterbury.org/articles.php/2512/archbishops-study-morning-university-of-warwick#sthash.AmKUVDKR.dpuf>

Introduction

We discover what's involved in our Christian commitment not (of course!) by reading books about it but by the daily effort to live in a way that allows Jesus Christ to come through in our lives; we are caught up in the task of showing that what we say is *credible*. And at the same time, it is this daily effort to be 'transparent' to Christ that teaches us all over again what it means to say that we are Christians.

So 'being disciples' means at least two things. It means very simply going on asking whether what we do, how we think and speak and act, is open to Christ and Christ's Spirit; developing the skills of asking ourselves the difficult questions about our consistency and honesty, about how seriously we take what we say. And it is also about how we as a Church go on being a *learning community*, how we grow in depth of relation with each other and God. The addresses collected in this little book – most of them originally delivered to audiences of lay Christians of all ages and backgrounds – are all in their different ways about these issues, and I hope very much that they may be a starting point for exploring ways in which we can go on growing in the life that Jesus shares with us, so that we can become signs of life and hope in our world. My thanks to those who listened to these talks and offered perspectives, comments and challenges that helped me see more clearly.

1

Being disciples

The next day John again was standing with two of his disciples, and as he watched Jesus walk by, he exclaimed, 'Look, here is the Lamb of God!' The two disciples heard him say this, and they followed Jesus. When Jesus turned and saw them following, he said to them, 'What are you looking for?' They said to him, 'Rabbi' (which translated means Teacher), 'where are you staying?' He said to them, 'Come and see.' They came and saw where he was staying, and they remained with him that day. It was about four o'clock in the afternoon.   (John 1.36–39)

Discipleship, as the title of this book indicates, is a state of being. Discipleship is about how we live; not just the decisions we make, not just the things we believe, but a state of being. It's very telling that, at the very beginning of John's Gospel (John 1.38–39), when the two disciples of John the Baptist come to Jesus they say, 'Rabbi, where are you staying?' Jesus says, 'Come and see', and they stay with him for the rest of the day. The Gospel teaches us that the bottom line in thinking about discipleship has something to do with this *staying*. Later on in the same Gospel (especially John 15) the same language of 'staying'

1

or 'abiding', as it is often translated, is used again to describe the ideal relation of the disciple to Jesus: 'Abide in me', he says; 'abide in my love' (John 15.4, 9).

In other words, what makes you a disciple is not turning up from time to time. Discipleship may literally mean 'being a student', in the strict Greek sense of the word, but it doesn't mean turning up once a week for a course (or even a sermon). It's not an intermittent state; it's a relationship that continues. The truth is that, in the ancient world, being a 'student' was rather more like that than it is these days. If you said to a modern prospective student that the essence of being a student was to hang on your teacher's every word, to follow in his or her steps, to sleep outside their door in order not to miss any pearls of wisdom falling from their lips, to watch how they conduct themselves at the table, how they conduct themselves in the street, you might not get a very warm response. But in the ancient world, it was rather more like that. To be the student of a teacher was to commit yourself to living in the same atmosphere and breathing the same air; there was nothing intermittent about it.

Being a 'disciple', a learner, in that sense is a state of being in which you are looking and listening without interruption. It's much more like, for instance, the condition of the novice monks we read about in the sayings of the Desert Fathers, who hang around hoping that they will get the point, occasionally saying desperately to the older monks, 'Give us a word, Father,' and at last the older monk says something really profound like, 'Weep for your sins,' followed by six weeks of silence. Or indeed the relationship between (even today) the Buddhist novice and the master in a Zen community, where something similar applies. You are hanging around; you are watching; you are absorbing a way of being that you are starting to share. You learn by sharing life; you learn by looking and listening.

So that little exchange at the beginning of John's Gospel ('"Rabbi, where are you staying?" . . . "Come and see." They came and saw where he was staying, and they remained with him that day') is quite a good beginning for thinking about discipleship. It's no accident that John puts it right at the beginning of his Gospel. If we're going to understand what he has to say to us about discipleship, we have to understand about abiding and sharing, this 'non-intermittent' quality in being a disciple.

Being aware and attentive

I shall have a little more to say about that sharing a place, an atmosphere, a state of being. But for now let's just stay with what it involves and think a little about discipleship as a state of *awareness*. The disciple is not there to jot down ideas and then go away and think about them. The disciple is where he or she is in order to be changed; so that the way in which he or she sees and experiences the whole world changes.

3

That great Anglo-Welsh poet David Jones wrote poignantly in one of his late poems about the poet's relation to God: 'It is easy to miss him at the turn of a civilization.' Discipleship as awareness is trying to develop those skills that help you *not* to miss God, to miss Jesus Christ, at the turn of a civilization, or anywhere else. Awareness, in this connection, is inseparable from a sort of *expectancy*, and that is one of the characteristics that most clearly marks the true disciple. Disciples are expectant in the sense that they take it for granted that there is always something about to break through from the Master, the Teacher, something about to burst through the ordinary and uncover a new light on the landscape. The Master is going to speak or show something; reality is going to open up when you are in the Master's company and so your awareness (as has often been said by people writing about contemplative prayer) is a little bit like that of a birdwatcher. The experienced birdwatcher, sitting still, poised, alert, not tense or fussy, knows that this is the kind of place where something extraordinary suddenly bursts into view.

I've always loved that image of prayer as birdwatching. You sit very still because something is liable to burst into view, and sometimes of course it means a long day sitting in the rain with nothing very much happening. I suspect that, for most of us, a lot of our experience of prayer is precisely that. But the odd occasions when you do see what

T. S. Eliot (in section IV of 'Burnt Norton') called 'the king-fisher's wing' flashing 'light to light' make it all worthwhile. And I think that living in this sort of expectancy – living in awareness, your eyes sufficiently open and your mind both relaxed and attentive enough to see that when it happens – is basic to discipleship.

Now, in the Gospels the disciples don't just listen, they are expected to *look* as well. They are people who are picking up clues all the way through. This is shown to us in very different ways in different Gospels, as the disciples of Jesus begin to understand things in different ways and at different speeds. So, for example, the Gospel of Mark tends to portray the disciples as incredibly stupid about picking up clues: they can't do it. The kingfisher flashes past them and Peter or someone (usually Peter) turns round and says, 'Oh, I missed that!' In contrast, John's Gospel presents us with a steady accumulation of moments of recognition and realization, from the moment (right after the first sign in Cana of Galilee) when the disciples 'see his glory' (John 2.11), and they begin to understand.

This theme of seeing comes to its great climax when (in chapter 20) Peter and the Beloved Disciple stumble into the empty tomb and see the folded grave clothes. It's an inexhaustibly wonderful text because it distinguishes so clearly between the first moment when Peter looks in and 'notices' and the other disciple comes in and 'sees'.

Indeed, you can draw up a chart of these words as they are used throughout the Gospel's narrative to pick out the stages and modes of noticing that John wants us to be conscious of as part of the disciple's task.

Not that the disciples always get it right even in John's accounts. They are still at times a bit slow, though not nearly as dim-witted as they sometimes appear in Mark. But this corresponds to dimensions of our own discipleship: those longish periods where, looking back, we feel, 'How could we have been so obtuse?' and those times where we think, 'Yes: I don't see it all yet but it's beginning to link up.' For me, as for so many, the excitement of reading John's Gospel in the context of trying to be a disciple is something to do with the exhilarating sense of things linking up as the great narrative unfolds. I'm sure that in reality Peter and John and the rest of the disciples were actually not so very different from us: that is, they had their dim-witted days – but also those days when things begin to join up and you see a hint of the overwhelming big picture that is being uncovered for you.

> *Disciples watch, they remain alert, attentive, watching symbolic acts as well as listening for instructive words*

Disciples watch, they remain alert, attentive, watching symbolic acts as well as listening for instructive words; watching the actions that give the clue to how reality is being reorganized around Jesus. Back to the early stages of John's story once again – the wedding at Cana (John 2.11): 'Jesus did this, the first of his signs, at Cana of Galilee, and revealed his glory; and his disciples believed in him'. The disciples see what's going on and something connects; they know that what is before them is worthy of commitment.

But sometimes those signs, those symbolic actions, are difficult or ambiguous. 'What did you do that for?' is a question that occasionally hangs around the Gospel narratives. There's the occasion in the Synoptic Gospels (Matthew 21.18–22; Mark 11.12–14, 20–25) of the cursing of the fig tree as Jesus goes to Jerusalem. The disciples' puzzlement at what's going on there is shared by many modern readers; but there it is, an action that Jesus, so to speak, offers to the disciples and says, 'What do you make of that? Do you see what that's about?'

Or again, we have another odd exchange in Mark 8 between Jesus and the disciples in the boat after the feeding of the crowd of four thousand. 'Don't you understand yet? Haven't you grasped it yet?' asks Jesus. He quizzes them about what they have seen in the feeding of the two great crowds of five thousand and four thousand, and ends, almost plaintively, 'So you still don't get it?' (Mark 8.21), The exact significance of this exchange continues to give biblical scholars headaches, but what matters for us now is that Jesus clearly requires awareness and expectancy in his disciples, watching the acts as well as listening to the words, watching with a degree of inner stillness that allows the unexpected world-changing flash of the kingfisher's wing to occur.

And for us today, trying to be Christ's disciples, awareness and expectancy are still central. We are not precisely where those first disciples were. We are post-resurrection believers and we ought to be able to understand a little more than Christ's first disciples in the Gospels did. In theory, at least. We have the Holy Spirit to direct and inform, to energize our awareness, to kindle our expectancy. Like those first disciples, we look as well as listen. We watch with expectancy the world in which we live. We listen for the word to come alive for us in Scripture. We look at the great self-identifying actions of the Church in the sacraments, asking the Spirit to make the connection come alive.

But not only that; we look at one another as Christians with expectancy – an aspect of discipleship that is not always easy to hold to. Yet it can't be said too often that the first thing we ought to think of when in the presence of another Christian individual or Christian community is: what is Christ giving me through this person, this group? Given that we may not always see eye to eye with other Christians we mix with, that can be hard work (and no doubt it's at least equally hard work for them looking at us). But, nonetheless, Jesus has brought us together precisely so that we approach one another with that degree of expectancy. It doesn't mean that you will agree with everything the other Christian says or does; simply that you begin by asking, 'What is Jesus Christ giving me here and now?' Never mind the politics, the hidden agenda, or anything else of that kind, just ask that question and it will move you forward a tiny bit in discipleship. Can we live in a Church characterized by expectancy towards one another of that kind? It would be a very deeply biblical and gospel-shaped experience of the Church if we could.

Being with Jesus

Awareness, expectancy, discipleship as a state of being – all of this is bound up with the idea of the disciple as some-one who *follows*. This listening awareness, this expectancy, presupposes following because it assumes that we are willing to travel to where the Master is, to follow where the Master goes. And, of course, in the Gospels, where the Master goes is very frequently not where we would have thought of going, or would have wanted to go. Hence the language of taking up the instrument of our execu-tion – the cross – and walking his way. Familiar and pious language, which we need to hear afresh as the chilling and sobering summons it really is.

9

Let's look at Luke 14 for a moment. In that chapter Jesus talks repeatedly and insistently about what sort of lives *cannot* be lived by disciples. They are very hard words. Those who come to Jesus cannot be his disciples unless they love him more than they love father and mother, wife and children, brothers and sisters (14.26). More than themselves as well: 'Whoever does not carry the cross and follow me cannot be my disciples' (14.27). This language of 'not being able' to be a disciple echoes through that chapter in a very alarming way. But the point is that if you are going to be where the Master is, those things you think come naturally and comfortably are not necessarily going to define where you find yourself. The place where you are going to be is always going to be defined by the Master, not by you or indeed, ultimately, by any of your qualities or relationships, because 'a disciple is not greater than his master', as both Luke and John tell us. Being with the Master is recognizing that who you are is finally going to be determined by your relationship with him. If other relationships seek to define you in a way that distorts this basic relationship, you lose something vital for your own well-being and that of all around you too. You lose the possibility of a love more than you could have planned or realized for yourself. Love God less and you love everyone and everything less.

Following so as to be in the same place as the Master: there are two very interesting and rather different directions in which we can take this idea. The first is a fairly obvious point, but one that is quite important in thinking about discipleship in the New Testament. Being where Jesus is means being in the company of the people whose company Jesus seeks and keeps. Jesus chooses the company of the excluded, the disreputable, the wretched, the self-hating, the poor, the diseased; so that is where you are going to find yourself. If you are going to be where

> *Being where Jesus is means being in the company of the people whose company Jesus seeks*

Jesus is, if your discipleship is not intermittent but a way of being, you will find yourself in the same sort of human company as he is in. It is once again a reminder that our discipleship is not about choosing our company but choosing the company of Jesus – or rather, getting used to the fact of having been chosen for the company of Jesus.

That is why so many great disciples of Jesus across the history of the Christian Church – and indeed now – find themselves in the company of people they would never have imagined being with, had they not been seeking to be where Jesus is: those who have gone to the ends of the earth for the sake of the gospel; those who have found themselves in the midst of strangers wondering, 'How did I get here?' People like Thomas French, a great missionary figure of the nineteenth century who spent much of his ministry as bishop in the Persian Gulf at a time when the number of Christians in the area was in single figures, and who died alone of fever on a beach in Muscat. What took him there? What else except the desire to be where Jesus was, the sense of Jesus waiting to come to birth, to come to visibility, in those souls whose lives he touched – even though, in the long years he worked in the Middle East he seems to have made no converts. He wasn't there first to make converts, he was there first because he wanted to be in the company of Jesus Christ – Jesus Christ reaching out to, seeking to be born in, those he worked with and loved so intensely. It's the apparent failure, and the drama of that failure, so like the 'failure' of Jesus abandoned on the cross, that draws me to his story, because it demonstrates what a discipleship looks like that is concerned with being where Jesus is, regardless of the consequences.

Being with the Father through the Son

There is another, deeper consequence of being with Jesus, a consequence that comes again and again into visibility in the Fourth Gospel. 'Where I am, there will my servant be also,' says Jesus (John 12.26). And where Jesus Christ is – so John has told us at the beginning of his Gospel – is 'close to the Father's heart' (John 1.18). The Word of God is 'in the bosom of the Father', as older translations have it. Where he is, we are to be also. We are to be where he is not only in terms of mission and outreach and service in the world, in serving and accompanying the outcast; we are also to be where he is in his closeness to the Father. We follow him, not simply to the ends of the earth, to do his work and echo his service; we follow him to be next to the heart of the Father.

There is a connection in John's Gospel between the way in which disciples are to see and do what their Master is doing, and what Jesus himself says about his relation to the Father. If you look at John 5.19–20, you find one of the Gospel's great affirmations of how the Son does what the Father is doing because the Son *sees* what the Father is doing. The Son gazes on and absorbs the eternal action of the Father, and acts it out in his own life, in eternity and in history. The Son, the Word of God, drinks in the everlasting act of the Father and then makes it real in another context. Does John mean us to pick up an echo of that in the places in his Gospel where he speaks in similar terms about our seeing and doing? As if the ground of our discipleship was ultimately the way in which the eternal Word and the eternal Source relate to each other?

Compare this with John 7.3: 'Leave here,' say Jesus' brothers, 'and go to Judea so that your disciples also may see the works you are doing; for no one who wants to be widely known acts in secret.' As usual, there is an irony here: Jesus will go to Jerusalem and act in public; but that act will finally be his agony and death. The disciples will *see* that his anguish and helplessness are his actions, even his divine actions. Likewise in the great meditations of the farewell discourses (particularly John 17), it is very clear that seeing what Jesus is doing in his Passion is crucial. The disciples see what Jesus is doing as he exposes himself to mortal risk, and they also see that he is doing what the Father is doing; they see the 'glory' that Jesus and the Father give to each other, and that glory is given to them. We are surely meant to make some connection between the seeing and doing of Jesus in relation to the Father, and the seeing and doing that goes on between disciples and Jesus. Jesus sees the Father and knows what he must do and suffer; and so his suffering becomes the action of God, not just a terrible historical disaster. The disciples are being prepared to see this glorious divine moment in the cross, and so to open their own human lives to the act of God, in joy and suffering alike.

This helps us again with what I called at the beginning of this chapter the 'non-intermittent' character of discipleship. The relationship of Jesus to the Father is not episodic. Jesus does not receive an occasional bit of instruction from the Father; his relationship is sustained, eternal and unbroken. He gazes into the mystery of the Father's love and he enacts it, in heaven and on earth. And so we in our discipleship are summoned to gaze into the mystery of that infinite love and to seek to do that same eternal will: to 'act' that same action, on earth as it is in heaven, as the Lord's Prayer puts it.

This suggests the rather ambitious thought (though it is an ambition entirely justified by Scripture) that the heart of discipleship is bound up with the life of the Trinity; as we develop our understanding of the trinitarian life of God, uncovered for us in those wonderful passages of John's Gospel, so we develop in our understanding of what provides the root and energy of our being disciples here and now. We see and we do, not just because that is the way discipleship or studentship worked in the ancient world; we see and we do because that is what the Father and the Son are involved in for all eternity.

Being and action

Let me try to draw some of this together. To get some perspective on the biblical sense of the disciples' identity means first and foremost the simple willingness to be consistently in Christ's company. What that means practically for the Christian today is seeking constantly the company of other servants of Christ, the company of the revelation of Christ in Scripture, the company of the Father and the Son, in the Spirit, in prayer. All of this requires of us a certain degree of inner stillness, a sort of poise: the attentiveness of the birdwatcher; attention and expectancy, an attitude of mind sufficiently free of the preoccupations of the ego to turn itself with openness to what God in Christ is giving.

At the primary level, that will mean learning and deepening our attentiveness to the Bible, to the sacraments and to the life of the Body of Christ. Second, arising out of that, it means learning a new level of attentiveness to all persons, places and things; looking at everything with the eye of expectancy, waiting for something of God to blossom within it; being in Christ's company, learning attentiveness and practising this kind of still alertness; looking and waiting for the light to break through. Third, it means being attentive to where Christ is going; keeping company with those he is with. Among them we will find the most unexpected and unlikely characters, the kinds of people Jesus seems to spend so much time with in the Gospels and today. Most importantly, we will find him keeping company with the Father, in whose company he eternally is.

So our attentiveness is not just a kind of aesthetic attitude, an appreciation of beauty. It is also a willingness to bring an active and transfiguring love into this situation of expectancy, to keep company so that an action and a relationship may come into being. Being disciples means being in his company; learning stillness, attentiveness, expectancy; being willing to go where Jesus is going and to be in the company of those he's in company with. And it means letting the action come through, letting the relation be made; letting Christ's action come through us as the Father's act comes through him.

What seems to be suggested by these reflections upon the biblical identity of the disciple is that our discipleship in the company of Jesus is a trinitarian mode of life, embedded in the relationship of the Father, the Son and the Holy Spirit: that is, it is a contemplative mode of life. Not in the sense that we should all become hermits, but we have got to grow into a mature stillness, a poise and an openness to others and the world, so that it can also be a transformative mode of living in which the act of God can come through, so as to change ourselves, our immediate environment, our world.

> *We have all got to grow into a mature stillness, a poise and an openness to others and the world*

A trinitarian living, a contemplative living, a transformative living: no opposition here (as there isn't in the Fourth Gospel) between contemplation and action. But one of the most awful clichés that Christians have sometimes been trapped by is the question of which matters more: contemplation or action. Perhaps the only decisive answer is that if you imagine contemplation without action or action without contemplation, you realize that you are drawing up a charter for really sterile, and potentially even destructive, human living. Hold them together – contemplation as an openness to the real roots of transforming action – and maybe it doesn't appear quite such a stand-off. The greatest teachers of prayer and action have held those together in the most remarkable way; like St Teresa of Avila (1515–82), saying that when you have finally 'progressed' through all the hair-raising mystical experiences she describes, what it's all finally about is enabling you to do some very ordinary things a little bit better, in a way that is suffused by eternal love taking up residence in the heart. (Or, by the time you have been through the seventh mansion of spiritual union with God, you are better at the washing-up.)

And so this habit of attentiveness and expectancy towards God and one another results, or overflows, in a mode of being and action in the world that – because it can be free from ego and anxiety – actually allow God-shaped change to take place around you. This happens not by effort and struggle, with furrowed brows and tensed muscles, but by allowing something to rise up, something irresistible within your awareness that is God's purpose coming through to make the difference that only God can make. A disciple is, as we have seen, simply a learner; and this, ultimately, is what the disciple learns: how to be a place in the world where the act of God can come alive.

For reflection or discussion

1 Where do you most often sense the company of Jesus?
2 Does your Christian community or congregation expect people to grow in understanding, and how does it help that to happen?

2

Faith, hope and love

Love never ends. But as for prophecies, they will come to an end; as for tongues, they will cease; as for knowledge, it will come to an end. For we know only in part, and we prophesy only in part; but when the complete comes, the partial will come to an end. When I was a child, I spoke like a child, I thought like a child, I reasoned like a child; when I became an adult, I put an end to childish ways. For now we see in a mirror, dimly, but then we will see face to face. Now I know only in part; then I will know fully, even as I have been fully known. And now faith, hope, and love abide, these three; and the greatest of these is love.

(1 Corinthians 13.8–13)

Faith, hope and love: three indispensable qualities in the life of the Christian disciple. But how do they work? And how can they best be nurtured? I want to explore those questions in a slightly roundabout way by approaching them as they are dealt with by one of the great mystics of Christian history, the sixteenth-century Spanish friar, St John of the Cross – mostly because of one very distinctive insight he has about them.

Like other theologians of his time, St John of the Cross takes for granted a picture of the human mind that sees it as working in three basic ways: the human mind *understands*, it *remembers* and it *wants*. Or, in more abstract terms, the human mind is made up of the interaction of understanding, memory and will. The distinctive and fresh insight that St John of the Cross offers is that if you put together understanding, memory and will with faith, hope and love, you have a perfect picture of where we start and where we finish. In the Christian life, faith (he says) is what happens to our understanding; hope is what happens to our remembering; and love is what happens to our wanting. So to grow as a disciple is to take the journey from understanding into faith, from memory into hope and from will into love.

> To grow as a disciple is to take the journey from understanding into faith, from memory into hope and from will into love

St John believed that in this process of Christian growing up, one of the most difficult things is the sense we will have that we have lost our bearings on the way. What we thought we understood we discover that we never did; what we thought we remembered is covered with confusion; and what we thought we wanted turns out to be empty. We have to be recreated in faith and hope and love for our understanding, our memory, and our will to become what God really wants them to be.

I'm going to use that structure as a way of getting into thinking about faith and hope and love, looking at some of the problems and crises that confront us in our contemporary culture in respect of our understanding, our remembering and our wanting – ways in which we try to deny or run away from the way the problem is posed; and how as disciples we can recover our direction and enter into the fullness of our humanity.

Faith and understanding

Let's begin with understanding, or intelligence. I'm tempted to say that at the moment we live in a culture where intelligence is not very much prized – but that is probably a bit of an overstatement and needs some explanation. The issue is how we *understand* things in an environment where we are spectacularly confused about what might be involved in claiming any interest in truth for its own sake. How does *intelligence* work in a culture where people are constantly asking, 'What is truth?' and 'Is there such a thing?' Because traditionally, intelligence has to do with the idea of a fitting or adequate relationship between the mind and what is beyond it; if there is no 'beyond', there is no fit. And this also means that there are no awkward questions to be asked as intelligence advances, because it doesn't in any interesting sense advance and generate new perspectives.

These days we have, very often, an approach to intelligence or knowledge that treats it in a robustly functional way. Take the kind of official document on the purpose of education that tells us that its primary aim is to make us a more competitive economy. Whatever that is about, I don't really think it's about intelligence. It's an approach that doesn't really seem to prize intelligence in the old sense; it doesn't give much scope for the mind to be stretched and challenged and enriched in completely unpredictable ways (indeed, in what may be completely unprofitable ways in terms of the visible measures of economic production).

Yet at the same time we have what we have learned to call the post-modern perspective, in which any one view may be as good as any other, and one person's claim to truth (let alone absolute truth) can be regarded by others as offensive or oppressive. We are in a period that St John of the Cross might well have described in his characteristic language as a 'dark night' for intelligence. We don't quite know what *knowing* is *for*, and we don't even know *that* we can know or *what* we can know. And this affects our Christian self-understanding as well. In the Western world believers have lost a great deal of doctrinal certainty, even if they talk about it loudly. There has been a loss of confidence in our ability to trace the works of God and boldly relay to the world what God has said. We sometimes deny this by adopting tribal, moralizing, noisy forms of faith, which insist that clarity can be attained and doubts silenced and which contrast themselves with the general atmosphere of loss of nerve; but these often fail to come to terms with the scale of the cultural change we inherit, and their very insistence becomes an unsettling sign of the new environment.

We seem to have lost our bearings. Of course, the Church at large continues to say what it has always said in the context of worship, and it reads its Bible faithfully; more than may be realized, this does just go on in countless individual Christian hearts and minds, which is all to the good. And yet in so much of the perceived and public life of the Church there seems to be a degree of loss of nerve and confidence. Can we really *understand* God? Can we really expect people to absorb the doctrinal universe with its full and rich pattern that an earlier generation inhabited so much more confidently? But in among all this is also a problem of a loss of confidence in *reason* in our contemporary world. By that I don't mean a loss of confidence in rational procedures so much as a loss of patience with argument, real mutual persuasion; a loss of the idea that by mutual persuasion and careful argument we might have our minds enlarged to receive more of the truth. Our intelligence is not in a very good state, it seems, either in or out of the Church. And we have devised a number of quite successful ways of pretending there isn't a problem.

Now, what St John of the Cross says to us – and he's not just writing for Carmelite nuns in sixteenth-century Spain – is that out of this sense of a 'brick wall' before our intelligence, this sense of confusion and loss where our understanding is concerned, *faith* grows in its true meaning. It appears not as a system, a comprehensive answer to all our problems. It appears quite simply in the form of 'dependable relationship'. You may not understand, or have the words on the tip of your tongue, but you learn somehow to be confident in a presence, an 'other', who does not change or go away. You realize that when the signposts and landmarks have been taken away there is a presence that does not let you go. And that is faith, I would say, in a very deeply biblical sense.

> *You learn somehow to be confident in a presence, an 'other', who does not change or go away*

Look at the disciples in the Gospels, and the number of times they fail to get the point and Jesus says, 'Don't even you understand?' Look at how often they ask the silly questions, the times when they try to turn away, when they manifestly don't know what's going on. But in the great words of Peter in John 6.68, they also say, 'To whom else can we go?' They know that the presence that has called them is dependable and that while they may be insecure, volatile, and easily capable of betrayal, forgetting and running away, what they confront in the person they call Rabbi and Master is one who will *not* go away.

The loss of understanding, of a clear sense of what we know and how we know, is part of the difficult business of learning to question at every level who we are. But we are somehow set free to face all that and live with it by the conviction that we are not 'let go' of. Faith as dependable relationship is something other than faith as a system of propositions, or faith as confidence in my own capacity to master truth; it's much more a confidence that *I can be* mastered by truth, that I can be held even when I don't feel I can hold on. If my relation with the living truth is initiated and sustained by God's faithfulness not mine, it is dependable. But recognizing that requires me to step back from confidence in my own resources.

So in our age, and in the age that lies ahead, the faith we as Christians proclaim will need to be not a clever system but the possibility of dependable relationship. We need to point quite simply to the God who does not let go, to the Christ who does not run away. And (here's the rub) we ourselves need to be dependable people – people in dependable relationship, who are there for those who feel abandoned and those who don't know who and where they are. By our faithfulness to the lost, the suffering and the marginal we begin to show what it is to have faith in the one who doesn't let go. And one of the biggest challenges to the Church today is how we embody that kind of dependability in this society and throughout the world. It may require a shift in the kind of Church we think we are, given that we are most commonly perceived (unfairly, no doubt, but pretty widely) as people who are anxious about who they should say 'no' to.

So there's the challenge: in the age of a dark night of the intelligence we are being nudged in the direction of understanding faith afresh in terms of dependable relation. We are drawn into it with God; and we are summoned to embody it and to offer it, as Christ's disciples.

Hope and memory

The dark night and the brick wall affect *memory* just as much. People sometimes speak about our social amnesia. Once every six months or so, one or other of the newspapers will start again asking the question, 'What is Britishness?', 'What are British values?', 'Have we forgotten our history?' and 'What's being taught in our schools about our heritage?' If the problem of intelligence is, 'What is truth?' the problem before our memory is, 'Have we forgotten who we were?' Crises of identity are common now in society, not just in individuals. What is it to be British? But for that matter, what is it to be Western? Christian? 'Modern'? What is it to be Muslim? Jewish?

The crises of identity for individuals are no less serious; and they have a very particular form in our age, coming into focus as crises about *continuity*: 'Am I the same person as I was?' In a culture where the average person is unlikely to have a job for life, and increasingly, sadly, not likely even to have a set of stable relationships for life, is there something that holds together the various coming-and-going experiences that enter into the mind and the psyche? Fractured careers and broken relationships seem to be the order of the day. Is there one story that can be told about who I am, and about who *we* are?

Just as with intelligence, so with memory; we find strategies of denial for Church, society and indeed individual. We can construct satisfying stories and recreate an imagined past. We can take refuge not in tradition (which is a good thing), but in an artificial traditionalism (which isn't). We can make up continuities and pretend they are there when they are not: a dark night of memory.

What would St John of the Cross say to all that? Hope, when it comes to birth, is not just a confidence that there is a future for us; it's also a confidence that there's a continuity such that the future is related to the same truth and living reality as the past and the present. Hope, like faith, is hope *in relation*; relation to that which does not go away and abandon, relation to a reality that knows and sees and holds who we are and have been. You have an identity not because you have invented one, or because you have a little hard core of selfhood that is unchanged, but because you have a witness of who you are. What you don't understand or see, the bits of yourself you can't pull together in a convincing story, are all held in a single gaze of love. You don't have to work out and finalize who you are, and have been; you don't have to settle the absolute truth of your history or story. In the eyes of the presence that never goes away, all that you have been and are is still present and real; it is held together in that unifying gaze – imagine a pile of apparently disparate, disconnected bits suddenly revealed as being held together by a string, twitched by the divine observer, the divine witness.

That is very abstract, and it's put much more vividly and personally in an extraordinary poem by Dietrich Bonhoeffer, the great German theologian and martyr, when he was in prison for his share in the plot to assassinate Adolf Hitler (Dietrich Bonhoeffer, *Letters and Papers from Prison*, London: SCM Press, 1971, pp. 347–8). Bonhoeffer writes, 'They often tell me/ I would step from my cell's confinement/ calmly, cheerfully, firmly,/ like a squire from his country-house' (Bonhoeffer was a man of rather aristocratic background and bearing). But the poem is about the great gulf between what 'they' see – a confident, adult, rational, prayerful, faithful, courageous person – and what he *knows* is going on inside; the weakness and the loss and the inner whimpering and dread. 'So which is me?' Bonhoeffer asks. Is it the person they see, or the person I know when I'm on my own with myself? And his answer is surprising and blunt: I haven't got a clue; God has got to settle that. I don't have to decide if I'm really brave or really cowardly, whether I'm really confident or really frightened, or both. Who I am is in the hands of God. And that, I would say, is the hope that St John of the Cross might be talking about. It goes beyond the assumption that I *am* only what I see or know. It tells me that I am more than I realize, in the eyes of God, for good or ill. It tells me to hope in 'what is unseen' (a good biblical phrase), in the one who doesn't need to be told about how human beings work because he knows the human heart (John 2.25).

I am more than I realize, in the eyes of God

Hope, then, is not simply confidence in *the future*; it is confidence that past, present and future are held in one relationship so that the confusions about memory – Who were we? Who was I? Who am I, and who are we? – become bearable because of the witness in heaven, a witness who does not abandon. This suggests that the Church needs to be marked by profound patience: patience with actual human beings in their confusions and uncertainties; patience in an environment when so much seems to be unclear and in danger of getting lost; patience in the sense that we realize it takes time for each one of us to grow up into Christ. And if it takes time for us, then it takes time for the Body, the community, to grow overall. Hope and patience belong together. Only a Church that is learning patience can proclaim hope effectively.

Love and want

And then, what about what we want? What about the will? In our culture we talk a great deal about choice. Sadly, what we often mean is not a great deal more than might be called the 'supermarket shelf' choice. There are a lot of *things* out there and I'm free to decide which I want. But this treats our will, our choosing, as a series of disconnected, fractured acts of choosing, expressions of the surface of what I want. I'll have that one, and not that one, but it doesn't much matter. What matters is that I'm 'free', here and now, to exercise my choice.

Somewhere in that kind of talk about freedom we lose touch with the sense of the deep desires that actually make us who we are. We lose touch with the sense that there is a current in our lives moving towards a goal. In a strange way, in this society we have underplayed the reality of *eros*. That sounds odd, because *eros*, in the form of sexual imagery, seems to be absolutely everywhere these days. But this is not the same as *eros* in the sense of the profound desire that makes me who I am, that makes the whole of my life drawn towards something beyond myself which gives meaning – the other person that I love, the God I seek to love. That sense of profound yearning for meaning and acceptance is by no means so clear in our society.

We privilege the consumer mentality ('I'll have that one') and so we fail to ask the deep questions about the direction of the desire at the root of our being. And we attempt to deal with this again by finding strategies that increase consumer choices in society, and so defer the awkward final question, 'What for?' Along with this are strategies that sharpen up our aggression and our self-assertion in individual contexts. We use the language of being 'purpose-driven' when often, alas, we just mean 'made capable of more aggressive assertion'. We market books about the secrets of successful people, which are mostly about the tactics of treading on the toes of others. We lose touch with the notion that the most important freedom is the freedom to be ourselves and the freedom to grow – not to 'be ourselves' in the sense of asserting what we want, moment by moment, but to discover slowly and patiently the deepest rhythms of our life, and to find the context in which we will grow as God means us to. Will and choice belong in that framework – not as acts of assertion, or choosing in a vacuum.

St John of the Cross would tell us that if we face the problems, if we confront the apparent 'dark night' around will and freedom and choice, and look hard at how we trivialize these realities in ourselves and in our culture, maybe we shall become ready to grow into love. Love: an expression of the freedom to receive. Love: that which drives us to take time and to let go of anxiety. Love: that which permits us to be enriched and to be 'given to', made alive, to be breathed into. Not a passive thing, as some of those images might suggest, but a state of openness to joy. Love: not simply as *doing good* but as a deep contemplative regard for the world, for humanity in general and for human beings in particular, and for God.

> *Love: that which permits us to be enriched and to be 'given to' – a state of openness to joy*

When St Paul writes about love in 1 Corinthians 13 he makes it very clear that love simply as 'doing good' isn't enough. Love has to be delight in another, the refusal to be glad at another's failure and the willingness to receive truth as a life-giving, joy-giving thing. Love is generated by being loved; it is not that we loved God, but that he loved us, says the first letter of John (1 John 4.10).

And that is where all the themes in this chapter come together. The dependable presence that doesn't go away; the presence that remembers and holds in a single gaze what has been true and is true of us; the eternal, unshakeable witness to what we are. That presence *is love.* We are seen, known and held, but above all we are welcomed. We are the objects of an eternal delight. And if that is sinking into our minds and hearts, then what the Church *is* fundamentally, and must show itself to be, is a place where time and space are given, where people are allowed the space to experience eternal love, a place where nothing needs to be left at the door and where people are made free to *receive* in a world that can seem to be *demanding* of them all the time – that they give, that they trade, that they offer, that they are out there making a difference. Is the Church an environment in which people can learn to open themselves to joy? The joy that can come only by letting ourselves go, and letting go of anxious selfishness and the obsession with constantly choosing.

Just as it is a great challenge for the Church to be a place that is dependable, a place that is patient, it is also a great challenge for the Church to become a place sufficiently still for people to open up, sufficiently quiet and unanxious for people to learn that they can receive what the ultimate truth of the universe wants to give them.

So these are some of the ways in which, in the midst of the anxieties and obsessions that characterize our age, we might come to rediscover the three 'theological virtues' of faith and hope and love. We rediscover them as we discover that relationship which makes us whole, that relationship with the unconditional presence and witness, absolution and affirmation that belong to God. We discover all this, in short, in relation to the God of the Gospels, the God of Jesus, the God Jesus is. The gospel of God, as the New Testament puts it before us, is good news about an eternal presence, an agency and intelligence wholly committed to who we are and who we shall become. It is wholly committed to our growth into what we are made to be, and to each person in our distinctiveness: patient, undemanding – and massively demanding. God offers us life, peace, presence to ourselves and to him; a gift that, in T. S. Eliot's words, costs us 'not less than everything', yet in another sense costs nothing at all, because gift is what it is.

Can we as disciples begin to speak of these things and show these things? Yes, if we are prepared to acknowledge our own denials, our sinful refusals of faith, hope and love; and if we are also prepared to do a bit of diagnosis of the denials of the society we live in, the denials that enslave us and trivialize our understanding and our remembering and our wanting. Yes, if we live consistently, courageously, in an awareness that the power that made us and redeemed us is a power devoted to the fullness of life.

Faith and hope and love: these three, says St Paul, are the heart of our discipleship, of our learning and growing in Christ. The greatest is love, because once we have understood the nature of that to which we are present in its eternal, unchangeable radiance and glory, everything else falls into place.

Faith and hope and love are the heart of our discipleship, of our learning and growing in Christ

For reflection or discussion

1 How have you coped with periods of dryness, frustration or emptiness in your life as a believer?

2 In what ways can churches help people resist the consumer mentality – in their approach to faith as well as their approach to other areas of life? How do churches themselves sometimes encourage such a mentality?

3

Forgiveness

> Ask, and it will be given to you; search, and you will find;
> knock, and the door will be opened for you. For everyone
> who asks receives, and everyone who searches finds, and
> for everyone who knocks, the door will be opened. Is there
> anyone among you who, if your child asks for bread, will
> give a stone? (Matthew 7.7–9)

Jesus speaks in Matthew's Gospel of how the human parent
will not give a child a stone when the child asks for bread.
If we ask for bread, the one thing that will persuade us
that the response is satisfactory is the knowledge that our
declaration of what we need has been heard, a knowledge
that comes as we know ourselves to be nourished. Part
of the nourishment we need is knowing that our sisters
and brothers in faith see and hear our needs *as they are*,
not as others imagine them to be. And the bread that is
shared among Christians is not only material resource but
the recognition of dignity. That difficult and inspiring
poet R. S. Thomas published a collection of poems in 1963
called *The Bread of Truth*; and to recognize human dignity
in one another is indeed to share the truth of what humanity
is in the eyes of God, the nourishment that truth gives.

We feed each other by honouring the truth of the divine image in each other.

The bread of forgiveness

If we pray, 'Give us this day our daily bread' with all this in mind, it becomes a prayer that asks God to sustain in us the sense of our humanity in its fullness and its richness; to give us those relations with other human beings that will keep us human, aware of our mortality and our need, yet nourishingly confident that we are loved. It is a prayer to be reminded of our need: let us never forget, we pray, that we *have* to be fed, and that we cannot generate for ourselves all we need to live and flourish. And at the same time, it is a prayer that we shall not be ashamed of our mortality, our physical and vulnerable being. We start from need – where else can we start? But that is a way into understanding how and why we matter, why we are valuable. The prayer poses a critical question to anyone who imagines that they can begin from a position of self-sufficiency; it affirms that to be in need of this 'bread of truth', in need of material or spiritual nurture, is in no way a failure but, on the contrary, a place of dignity. The prayer both challenges the arrogance of those who think they are not in need and establishes that the needy are fully possessed of a treasure that needs to be uncovered and released – the humanity that draws them into mutual relation.

Part of what we are praying for in these words is the grace to receive our own humanity as a gift. We ask for openness and gratefulness to whoever and whatever awakens us to our dignity and helps us realize that, while our dignity is essentially and primarily given in our creation, it is always in need of being called into active life by relation, by the gift of others. And the implication is clear that we should, in doing this, pray to be kept awake to what we owe to the neighbour in terms of gift; their humanity depends on ours as ours does on theirs.

Many commentators on the Lord's Prayer, such as Gregory of Nyssa, underline the irrationality of praying for our daily bread while then seeking to hold on to it at the expense of others. In the framework I have been outlining, this can be by way of a concern for *defending* my own dignity rather than being willing to receive it in love. Praying for our daily bread is asking to be reacquainted with our vulnerability, to learn how to approach not only God but each other, with our hands open. So to pray this prayer with integrity, we need to be thinking about the various ways in which we defend ourselves against the need to open our hands. We cannot fully and freely pray for our daily bread when we are wedded inseparably to our own rightness or righteousness, any more than we can when we are wedded to our own security or prosperity. And perhaps this explains why the Lord's Prayer at once goes on to pray for *forgiveness* – or rather for the gift of being forgiven as we have learned to forgive.

The person who asks forgiveness has renounced the privilege of being right or safe; she has acknowledged that she is hungry for healing, for the bread of acceptance and restoration to relationship. But equally the person who forgives has renounced the safety of being locked into the position of the offended victim; she has decided to take the risk of creating afresh a relationship known to be capable of involving hurt. Both the giver and the receiver of forgiveness have moved out of the safety zone; they have begun to ask how to receive their humanity as a gift.

Forgiveness is one of the most radical ways in which we are able to nourish one another's humanity. When offence is given and hurt is done, the customary human response is withdrawal, the reinforcing of the walls of the private self, with all that this implies about asserting one's own humanity as a possession

> Forgiveness is one of the most radical ways in which we are able to nourish one another's humanity

rather than receiving it as gift. The unforgiven and the unforgiving cannot see the other as people who are part of God's work of bestowing humanity on them. To forgive and to be forgiven is to allow yourself to be humanized by those whom you may least want to receive as signs of God's gift; and this process is deeply connected with the prayer for daily bread. To deny the possibilities of forgiveness would be to say that there are those I have no *need* of because they have offended me, or because they have refused to extend a hand to me.

A willingness to forgive is clearly the mark of a humanity touched by God – free from anxiety about identity and safety, free to reach out into what is other, as God does in Jesus Christ. But it may be that a willingness *to be forgiven* is no less the mark of a humanity touched by God. It is a matter of being prepared to acknowledge that I cannot grow or flourish without restored relationship, even when this means admitting the ways I have tried to avoid it, admitting sin. When I am forgiven by the one I have injured, I accept both that I have damaged a relationship, and that change is possible. And if the logic of the Lord's Prayer is correct, this acceptance arises from and is strengthened by our own freedom to bring about the change that forgiveness entails.

Forgiveness is the exchange of the bread of life and the bread of truth; it is the way in which those who have damaged each other's humanity and denied its dignity are brought back into a relation where each feeds the other and nurtures their dignity. It is a gross distortion of forgiveness that sees it as a sort of claim to power over another – being a patron or a benefactor towards someone less secure. We should rather think of those extraordinary words in the prophecy of Hosea (11.8–9) about the mercy of God: 'How can I give you up, Ephraim? . . . for I am God and not a mortal.' To forgive is to share in the *helpless-ness* of God, who cannot turn from God's own nature: not to forgive would be for God a wound in the divine life itself. Not power, but the powerlessness of the God whose nature is love is what is shown in

> To forgive is to share in the helplessness of God, who cannot turn from God's own nature

the act of forgiving. The disciple rooted in Christ shares that powerlessness, and the deeper the roots go the less possible it is not to forgive.

At the same time, to *be* forgiven is another kind of powerlessness – recognizing that I cannot live without the word of mercy; I cannot complete the task of being myself without the healing of what I have wounded. Neither the forgiver nor the forgiven can acquire a power that simply cuts off the past and leaves us alone to face the future: both have discovered that their past, with all its shadows and injuries, is now what makes it imperative to be reconciled, so that they may live more fully from and with each other.

The bread of tomorrow

Scholars at least since the time of St Jerome have worried over the odd Greek word that is used in the Gospels for 'daily bread' – *epiousios*, whose exact meaning has proved elusive. Jerome rendered it with grim literalism as

41

'supersubstantial' – not a very helpful translation, and one that has not survived, even in liturgical Latin, but it has prompted a good many fanciful speculations. It probably means simply 'the food on which we subsist'. But Jerome himself refers to an ancient Aramaic version which presented the prayer as 'Give us today the bread of tomorrow.' *If* that represents what Jesus said, then he was telling us to pray for the gifts of the coming kingdom to be received in the present. And if so, all that has been said so far is cast in a new light. The need, the hunger, we must learn to express is a need not simply for sustenance but for God's future. What we need is the new creation, the bread that comes down from heaven and gives life to the world.

This suggests a still closer connection between the prayer for daily bread and that for forgiveness. Mutual reconciliation is one of the marks of the work of the Spirit, a radically new possibility opened up through the Body of Christ: it is itself a sign of God's future at work, and so an instance of 'tomorrow's bread'. To put it more fully, the unveiling of our mutual need and the shared recognition of human dignity as something realized in communion are dimensions of our human experience in which God's future is visible. And where these things happen, whether or not they are named in the context of Christ and his Spirit, there is something of the sacramental reality of 'tomorrow's bread' – 'five minutes of heaven', to borrow the title of an English television drama (based on real events) which explored the cost of reconciliation in the setting of Northern Ireland. If forgiveness is the most demanding instance of learning to offer one's resources for the sake of the dignity of another, in many ways the least 'natural' or most counter-cultural form of service to each other, it is surely right to see it as a gift from the future, as God's undefeated purpose for us draws us forward.

'Give us this day our daily bread' is, then, a prayer that inevitably looks beyond the present moment and the settling of immediate needs – though at the same time it forbids being *anxious* about tomorrow. It is as if in order to live in peace and hope today, we have to ask for that foretaste or 'advance payment' of God's future which Paul identifies as the Holy Spirit (2 Corinthians 5.5, cf. Ephesians 1.14). It has been said that every petition in the Lord's Prayer is implicitly a prayer for the coming of the Spirit (several of the Early Fathers noted the ancient variant of 'Thy Kingdom come' as 'May thy Holy Spirit come'), and this is no exception. Praying for the Spirit is indeed praying for the grace to receive our humanity from God at each other's hands in the reality of communion – with all the struggle that this involves in turning towards the reality of the other, not remaining content with our images of each other. Becoming bread for each other means breaking the stony idols of ourselves and the other.

But to speak in these terms of bread and forgiveness and the future presses us towards thinking about the act in which Christians clearly set forth these realities as the governing marks of Christian existence: the Lord's Supper, the Eucharist. We celebrate this Supper until Christ comes, invoking the Spirit of the coming age to transform the matter of this world into the sheer gift of Christ to us, and so invoking the promise of a whole world renewed, perceived and received as gift. This is, supremely, tomorrow's bread. But it is so, of course, not as an *object* fallen from heaven, but precisely as the bread that is actively shared by Christ's disciples; and it is eaten both as an anticipation of the communion of the world to come and as a memorial of the betrayal and death of Jesus. That is to say, it is also a sacrament of forgiveness; it is the risen Jesus returning to his unfaithful disciples to create afresh in them this communion of the new world. The Eucharist is our symbol of what it would mean for the Lord's Prayer to be answered fully: God feeding his people through the death and resurrection of Jesus, which establishes that new community of the Spirit in which forgiveness is the common currency.

For reflection or discussion

1 Spend a bit of time thinking through an experience of profound hurt and how you have coped with it or are

coping with it. What sort of things have made it harder or easier to manage?

2 Think of a moment when you have experienced *being* forgiven: how does it change the way you see yourself and others?

4

Holiness

Now the Lord is the Spirit, and where the Spirit of the Lord is, there is freedom. And all of us, with unveiled faces, seeing the glory of the Lord as though reflected in a mirror, are being transformed into the same image from one degree of glory to another; for this comes from the Lord, the Spirit . . . For it is the God who said, 'Let light shine out of darkness', who has shone in our hearts to give the light of the knowledge of the glory of God in the face of Jesus Christ.   (2 Corinthians 3.17–18; 4.6)

If you look up 'holy' in a Bible dictionary, you are likely to get a strong impression that, at least in the Old Testament, being holy means being set apart, and it's also very much to do with being on rather dangerous territory. Remember, when Moses meets God at the burning bush, God says, 'Take your shoes off. This is holy ground.' And when the people of Israel come to Mount Sinai, they are told not to get too close because it's holy and so it's very, very dangerous. It's a bit like those notices on electricity pylons, warning of 'Danger of Death' with the rather vivid picture of a little cartoon figure with a sort of bolt of lightning going through them. That is what holiness often appears to mean in the Old Testament, and it's perhaps why one common response to talk about holy places or holy people is to run a mile.

If you turn to the New Testament, at first sight there is a bit of a contrast. For one thing, St Paul, when he begins his letters, often addresses the people to whom he's writing as 'holy' people: to the saints, to the holy people at Corinth, the holy people at Philippi. And that might give us a bit of a pause to start with, because it doesn't sound from the way that Paul uses that word, or the way it plays out in his letters, as though 'holy' there means dangerous and forbidding, as it seems to in parts of the Old Testament.

Another crucial passage that turns around our thinking on this is in John's Gospel (17.17), where Jesus says to his disciples at the Last Supper that he's just about to consecrate or sanctify himself; he's just about to 'make himself holy', and he wants his disciples to be holy in the same way. What this means is that Jesus is making himself holy by stepping forward towards his death, towards the cross. And the New Testament makes it very clear in a number of passages that the crucifixion is in one sense the supremely holy thing – the holiest event that ever happens – and yet it's found outside conventional holy places and a long way from conventionally holy people. It's an execution machine on a rubbish dump outside the city wall. Holiness in the New Testament is a matter of Jesus going right into the middle of the mess and the suffering of human nature. For him, being holy is being absolutely involved, not being absolutely separated.

We could spend the rest of this book exploring why the Old Testament and the New Testament ideas are not

Being holy is being absolutely involved, not being absolutely separated

nearly as contradictory as all this might suggest; but it's a helpful contrast to start with, simply because quite a lot of people have a feeling that 'holy' is a scary word for scary realities – that 'holy' is dangerous and weird. Of course, it's equally true that the word is often heard as suggesting something less robust or three-dimensional than ordinary life: 'holy' is to do with a particular kind of religious building, with dimmed religious light, or with people a bit drained of blood – the sort you see in some stained-glass windows. But whether we are thinking of dangerously weird or ghostly and vague, what these views have in common is the assumption that 'holy' is – well, in a nutshell, not like us.

This is where the way that Jesus talks about holiness at the Last Supper is so transforming. Holiness there is seen as going into the heart of where it's most difficult for human beings to be human. Jesus goes 'outside the city'; he goes to the place where people suffer and are humiliated, the place where people throw stuff out, including other people. 'Outside the camp', in the language of the Old Testament (also Hebrews 13.13). If we take this seriously, the Christian idea of holiness is to do with going where it's most difficult, in the name of Jesus who went where it was most difficult. He wants us to be holy like that.

That is why there is no contrast, no tension really, between holiness and involvement in the world. On the contrary, the most holy, who is Jesus, is the most involved, most at the heart of human experience. And we really misunderstand the whole thing very seriously if we think that holiness means being defended from our own humanity or other people's humanity: quite the opposite. To understand this, we need to bear in mind an all-important distinction between being holy and simply being good. There's a fine phrase in one of Evelyn Waugh's novels, when a character is described by another: 'She was saintly, but she wasn't a saint.' The character in question is indeed saintly, very strict, devout and intense, but the effect she has on those around her is to make them feel guilty, frustrated and unhappy. They feel inadequate, and I suspect that many of us experience this when we encounter people we think are saintly or Very Good – they make us feel rather worse (I had a Northern Irish friend when I was an undergraduate who said of a common acquaintance of ours, 'He's so nice you could kick him').

In contrast, *holy* people, those who are saints rather than saintly, actually make you feel better than you are. The pursuit of goodness can be experienced as if you are taking part in a competitive examination in which some people are scoring very well, others are on the borderline, and some are sinking below the line. But the holy person somehow enlarges your world, makes you feel more yourself, opens you up, affirms you. They are not in competition; they are not saying, 'I've got something you haven't.' They are showing us something that it's wonderful simply to have in the world.

When I think of the people in my own life that I call holy, who have really made an impact, it's this that comes across most deeply in them all. These people have made me feel better rather than worse about myself. Or rather, not quite that: these are never people who make me feel *complacent* about myself, far from it; they make me feel that there is hope for my confused and compromised humanity. God is big enough to deal with and work with actual compromised and imperfect people. Look! Here is a life in which he has come alive. Real holiness somehow brings into my life this sense of opening up opportunity, changing things. It's not about my being made to feel inadequate, or looked down on. On the contrary, somehow I feel a little bit more myself: not in any way that suggests I don't need to change, to 'repent and believe', but simply through recognizing God active in the world.

(I have a theory, which I started elaborating after I had met Archbishop Desmond Tutu a few times, that there are two kinds of egotists in this world. There are egotists that are so in love with themselves that they have no room for anybody else, and there are egotists that are so in love with themselves that they make it possible for everybody else to be in love with themselves. They are at home in their skins. It doesn't mean that they are arrogant or self-obsessed or think they are faultless. They have learned to sense some of the joy that God takes in them. And in that sense Desmond Tutu manifestly loves being Desmond Tutu; there's no doubt about that. But the effect of that is not to make me feel frozen or shrunk; it makes me feel that just possibly, by God's infinite grace, I could one day love being Rowan Williams in the way that Desmond loves being Desmond Tutu . . .)

That is one key aspect of holiness – which is why, in the Roman Catholic Church, one of the criteria used for making people saints is that they produce joy around them. This was put very well in a reminiscence about a great Anglican priest of about half a century ago. The woman described her first meeting with this priest, and said that as she talked to him the landscape changed, 'with a new light on it'. That seems to me a brilliant definition of what it's like to meet a holy person: the landscape changes with a new light on it. A holy person makes you see things in yourself and around you that you had not seen before; that is to say, enlarges the world rather than shrinking

> *A holy person makes you see things in yourself and around you that you had not seen before*

it. This is why we say of Jesus that he is the 'most Holy One', because he above all changes the landscape, casts a new light on everything. You can't look at anything the same way afterwards. As Paul says in his second letter to Corinth, when we're in Jesus Christ there's a new creation (2 Corinthians 5.17); nothing looks the same.

So we're beginning to build up a picture of holiness. It's not an extra special kind of goodness, because somehow it's not about competing levels of how good you are. It's about enlarging the world, and about being involved in the world. A holy person is somebody who is not afraid to be at the tough points in the centre of what it's like to be a human being; someone who, in the middle of all that, actually makes you see things and people afresh. At the end of the day, this boils down to something extremely simple and extremely difficult, which is that holy people, however much they may enjoy being themselves, are not obsessively interested in themselves. They allow you to see not them, but the world around them. They allow you to see not them, but God. You come away from them feeling not, 'Oh, what a wonderful person,' but, 'What a wonderful world,' 'What a wonderful God,' or even, with surprise, 'What a wonderful person I am too.'

That is the transforming thing, the acid test for identifying where holiness is. And the difficult thing, of course, is that you can't really do this by trying. If you sit down and say, 'I'm going to be completely unselfish and unselfconscious; every 20 minutes I shall check whether I'm being self-conscious, whether I'm being selfish; every 20 minutes I'll think whether I'm thinking . . . oh, hang on; that's the problem!' That is the catch in Christian holiness; it happens when you are not thinking about you, which is why there are no useful self-help books on being holy. There are self-help books on being thin, self-help books on being an effective leader, and on being a good cook, but I have yet to see a convincing self-help book on being a saint, and I would be very suspicious of any claims for one. Becoming holy is being so taken over by the extraordinariness of God that *that* is what you are really interested in, and that is what radiates from you to reflect on other people.

> Becoming holy is being taken over by the extraordinariness of God

There's the catch: if you want to be holy, stop thinking about it. If you want to be holy, look at God. If you want to be holy, enjoy God's world, enter into it as much as you can in love and in service. And who knows, maybe one day someone will say of you, 'You know, when I met them, the landscape looked different.'

And what goes for individual disciples goes for the Church itself. Every so often people come up with wonderful schemes for making the Church a holier place, which usually means making sure that some people don't get in, or some people who are in get out. We might think that a holy Church must be a Church that is full of people a bit like me at my best. But when the Church tries to become holy in that way it almost always ends up in an appalling mess. Exclusive, anxious and self-conscious. Am I really being conscientious enough, am I really being pure enough? Are *they* really being pure enough? Surely not! Whereas the truly holy Church is taken over by the excitement of the extraordinariness of God; it wants to talk about the beauty and splendour of God, and to show the self-draining, self-forgetting love of God by being at the heart of humanity, by being where people are most human.

Being holy is certainly being unselfish, but not (once again) in the sense of having a *policy* about how to become unselfish; it is being so interested in God and the world that you don't really have too much time to brood on yourself. We are all called to it, and we are all in Jesus' Spirit empowered for it, because the Spirit of Jesus is the Spirit that constantly renews in us the ability to pray with integrity and conviction; to pray to God intimately, as to a parent; to say 'Abba, Father.'

Paul says that the Lord, who is 'the Spirit', uncovers our faces and allows us to be transformed 'from one degree of glory to another' (2 Corinthians 3.16–18). The Spirit is peeling off the layers of illusion and defensiveness, so we can see things as they really are. And this means that a really holy person is someone like a great artist or musician or poet. They help us to see what we would otherwise miss: dimensions and depths in the world that we might not otherwise spot. Not every artist is a saint, by any manner of means. Some of them are conspicu-ously selfish egotists in their personal lives. But somehow in their *work* they forget themselves enough for something to come alive, to come through. And the saint, the holy person, is somebody who has been enabled to create that kind of artwork out of their very lives, to let something come through, to let a bigger world appear, a new light and a new landscape.

We start, then, on the path of holiness, with two very simple things – 'simple' in this case meaning 'difficult', as we have seen: *looking* – looking at Jesus, looking at what God is like, looking at the gospel, and all that that means; and *exploring* – exploring where human beings are, what their needs are, what they are calling us to do, how we may help make them more human. These two – looking at Jesus and exploring in the human world around you – are the only things that could possibly give any foundational advice on being holy, which, as I say, doesn't really work anyway. But start there, and who knows?

For reflection or discussion

1 Have you met anyone who strikes you as holy? What sort of things would lead you to think of a person in those terms?

2 Do you think of yourself as someone called to be 'holy'?

5

Faith in society

For just as the body is one and has many members, and all the members of the body, though many, are one body, so it is with Christ. For in the one Spirit we were all baptized into one body – Jews or Greeks, slaves or free – and we were all made to drink of one Spirit. Indeed, the body does not consist of one member but of many. If the foot were to say, 'Because I am not a hand, I do not belong to the body', that would not make it any less a part of the body. And if the ear were to say, 'Because I am not an eye, I do not belong to the body', that would not make it any less a part of the body. If the whole body were an eye, where would the hearing be? If the whole body were hearing, where would the sense of smell be? But as it is, God arranged the members in the body, each one of them, as he chose. If all were a single member, where would the body be? As it is, there are many members, yet one body. The eye cannot say to the hand, 'I have no need of you', nor again the head to the feet, 'I have no need of you.' On the contrary, the members of the body that seem to be weaker are indispensable, and those members of the body that we think less honourable we clothe with greater honour, and our less respectable members are treated with greater respect; whereas our more respectable members do not need this. But God has so arranged the body, giving the greater honour to the inferior member, that there may be no dissension within the body, but the members may have the same care for one another. If one member suffers, all suffer together with it; if one member is honoured, all rejoice together with it.   (1 Corinthians 12.12–26)

What place does Christian discipleship have in a modern democratic society? For many people, especially in Europe, there is a simple answer: its place is in private. A modern society naturally takes it for granted that people are free to believe and practise what they wish; so if they decide to believe and practise Christianity, or any other religion, that is their affair. But this freedom is no different from their freedom to buy what they like or wear what they like. It is an individual matter and should not affect the way they act as citizens in their society. And it is unthinkable that the law of their society should favour any one set of religious opinions, any more than it should give a special place to a particular set of preferences in artistic taste, food, clothes or cars. Religion may be respected in a general sort of way, and defended as a right by the law, but it does not belong in the sphere of public decision-making and policy.

This kind of secular approach has its origins in the European Enlightenment of the seventeenth and eighteenth centuries. After a period of savage religious wars, there was a strong and understandable desire to avoid further conflict over religion, and a deep suspicion of religious authority as oppressive and irrational. Many intellectuals believed that moral behaviour, combined with a vague reverence for a supernatural creator, was something that all reasonable people were capable of grasping and putting into practice; they did not need revelation from heaven, or religious institutions with priests and sacred books to tell them what they could work out for themselves. Religious authorities had no place in the government of a country.

As the modern age developed, a further element came to play a part in this. The idea of human rights became increasingly powerful. For many if not most who thought about it, this meant that each human individual was born with an intrinsic claim to be treated with respect, possessed of a natural dignity and liberty that should be recognized by the law. That liberty was essentially a freedom to choose what would make the individual contented; it was obviously limited by considerations of harm to others. A reasonable and fair society would be one in which each person's freedom to choose and to pursue their happiness was respected and each person was protected from being seriously disadvantaged by someone else exercising their freedom. This became an important aspect of modern capitalism, with its goal of increasing every individual's range of personal choices.

So the ingredients developed of a particular kind of modern secularism. On the basis of what I have been describing, the ideal society appears as one in which the government as a whole does not promote the values of any one philosophy or religion, except to affirm universal human rights to free choice; it does not give public recognition or support or privilege to any religious body, though it allows religions to exist as private associations, so long as they do not threaten the way in which society overall carries on its business. In different degrees, this is the assumption behind several modern societies: France is the clearest example, but the USA, despite its high level of religious practice, is in theory committed to this as well. Other countries – Britain, Germany, Italy, for example – have a more complicated position in that there is still a measure of public recognition for religion, and for Christian principles and values in particular. There is, however, fierce debate about whether that is a good thing in contemporary circumstances.

How does this affect the Christian disciple? I'll begin to answer that by making some observations about two particular concerns that political commentators regularly raise about this basic model of a 'secular' society, and how it functions. The first of these concerns, often raised by left-wing commentators, is that the market, while obviously the main organ by which any society secures and develops its common prosperity, does not ensure anything like an equitable distribution of resources. Both within particular societies and between different nations, damaging inequalities have grown, to the extent that they begin to affect the proper functioning of societies themselves. We are more aware than ever of the difficulties of securing real fairness in trade conditions for countries that have never had a foot on the ladder of the world economy.

A second concern, often pointed out by conservative critics, is that when our culture is so full of the language of relative values and so obsessed with consumerist patterns of behaviour, it is not clear where people can find the motivation to act for the sake of others or simply to value things – and people – that are not of immediate economic use. Until fairly recently, the inequalities of society were made less stark by the networks of voluntary agencies and charities that cared for those who were overlooked and damaged by wider social processes. But our age is one in which the spirit of volunteering often receives less encouragement. What is more,

If society has no moral orientation by which to guide younger citizens, what will fill the gap?

if society has no moral orientation by which to guide younger citizens, what will fill the gap? As stable patterns of family life are undermined by the same short-term consumerism that prevails in economics, as people become less willing or psychologically able to make the long-term and unconditional commitments of marriage and parenting, we cannot assume that children will grow up with clear moral priorities. And the effect on the young, as recent studies in the UK have shown with alarming clarity, is to produce a generation not of free spirits but of young people often bored and unhappy in a new and worrying way, vulnerable to mental illness as never before.

The rational philosophy of the last couple of centuries has been weakened. One of the paradoxes is that many people now mistrust and undervalue science almost as much as they do religion, because they do not take for granted the same confident attitude to reason and objective argument. And because advances in scientific and technological have brought their own nightmares and crises – nuclear warfare, genetic engineering, environmental pollution – it is not surprising that this mistrust is widely felt. The philosophy of human rights remains the cornerstone of so much of what we do in our legal systems; but we are more aware of the clash of competing rights, the risks of individualism, the assumption that I can always enforce what I believe is due to me. We are beginning to see that these things create a society that is aggressive and suspicious, where trust is in short supply.

We cannot turn the clock back; and I don't believe we can or should suppose that a society run according to strict religious principles would be happier or easier.

Traditional Muslims can and do argue that in the muddle and fragmentation of Western societies, only Islam is able to weld a cohesive society together in our present chaos. But it is not as though a single clear system of Islamic government exists that can be persuasively presented to the world; and the difficulties Muslim legal scholars often have about the limits to freedom of public religious diversity leave a question about how much of our conventional understanding of human rights is compatible with some strict Islamic legal philosophies.

But what the dialogue with Islam has done is to remind people in our Western societies that not everyone in the world simply takes for granted the same 'rational' and secular basis for social life. And if we disagree with the Islamic analysis, what have we to offer in its place as the basis for a moral society? I want to suggest here that there are two principles of Christian faith and discipleship that we need to form part of that basis: we are each of equal value to God, and we are all dependent on each other. We cannot do without them if we are ever to secure true justice and lasting peace and stability.

We are each of equal value to God

For the Christian disciple, human dignity – and therefore any notion of human rights – depends upon the recognition that every person is related to God before they are related to anything or anyone else. God has defined who they are and who they can be by his own eternal purpose, which cannot be altered by any force or circumstance in this world. People may refuse their calling or remain stubbornly unaware of it; but God continues to call them and to offer them what they need to fulfil their calling. And the degree to which that calling is answered or refused has consequences for eternity.

This means that whenever I face another human being, I face a mystery. There is a level of their life, their existence, where I cannot go and which I cannot control, because it exists in relation to God alone – a secret word he speaks to each one, whether they hear or refuse to hear, in the phrase from the prophecy of Ezekiel. The reverence I owe to every human person is connected with the reverence I owe to God, who brings them into being and keeps them in being. I stand before holy ground when I encounter another person – not because they are born with a set of legal rights which can be demanded and enforced, but because there is a dimension of their life I shall never fully see; the dimension where they come forth from the purpose of God into the world, with a unique set of capacities and possibilities. The Christian disciple will have the same commitment to human rights and human dignity; but they will have it

Whenever I face another human being, I face a mystery

because of this underlying reverence, not because of some legal entitlement.

It means that there are no superfluous people, no 'spare' people in the human world. Everyone is needed for the good of all. Human failure is tragic and terrible because it means that some unique and unrepeatable aspect of God's purpose has been allowed to vanish. As the great Russian novelist Boris Pasternak makes one of his characters say in *Doctor Zhivago*, we can easily forget how the empires of the ancient world simply assumed that vast numbers of human beings could be sacrificed and slaughtered without a second thought; but the Christian gospel declares that there is nothing more Godlike and precious than a single human person.

It means, therefore, that a human person is worth extravagant and lasting commitment. A human being deserves complete attention and care, whether rich or poor, whether they will live for a day or for nine decades.

It is typical of Christian practice, for example, that the dying receive costly and devoted care, and that those who do not have 'productive' mental capacities, as we usually understand them, are treasured – and that children and even the unborn are regarded with respect. And it is also typical of Christian practice, when it is vital and energetic, that people feel able to make the lifelong commitment of marriage to each other – because the beloved person will never be completely understood or 'captured', even in decades of relationship. The transient force of sexual attraction is in this way transfigured by a sense of the uniquely personal, and something radical and exciting becomes possible. Our crisis in sexual morality in the developed world is not just about a failure to keep rules; it is about a loss of the sense of personal mystery and the calling to explore and enjoy someone else's mysteriousness for a lifetime.

This principle also means that no one's value can be measured simply by how successful or how productive they are. There will always be something precious that does not need to be proved by success, something that escapes what society expects or demands. At the highest this may be the special calling of the artist; but it can also mean the respect and care given to all those who do not fit into the expectations of an increasingly impatient and demanding culture, with its obsessive overwork and consequent stress. The Christian vision of persons who are related to God before anything or anyone else represents a way of truly valuing work and patience, but also of valuing leisure and the capacity to receive as well as give.

No one's value can be measured simply by how successful or how productive they are

If our developed societies are marked by the tendency to ignore the uniqueness of individuals, to load ever more demands for work and measurable production on to them, to glamorize success and despise failure, and to turn sex into a recreation instead of lasting creative partnership, the Christian disciple will say: 'All this is a predictable result of abandoning the belief that each person is the work of God.' And we can go further than this – because God's creation is wider than the human race. What is true of persons is also true of things. Some early theologians of the Eastern Church spoke of each element in the material world carrying a 'word' from God, revealing an aspect of God's life and wisdom. If we believe this, we shall not be inclined to treat the world around us as if it were just a quarry from which we take what we want and exploit it. In the sphere of ecology and the crisis of our environment, we are now more than ever conscious of the need for something like a religious perspective to be brought back into our attitude to a world that is not ours but – once again – is related to God before it is related to us. In the Bible, God calls the world good before human beings are in it.

We are all dependent on each other

All this is a substantial enough picture of what Christian faith and discipleship brings to our attitudes to social life. And thus far it is still quite close to what a Jew or a Muslim or a Hindu might say, despite its clear foundation in the teaching of Jesus. People of many faiths can share these ideas and work on them together in society. But there is an extra element brought by Christianity to the creation of a good society, and this is the second principle I want to underline.

The New Testament describes what happens when human beings are brought into relationship with Jesus Christ by faith as a community in which everyone's gifts are set free for the service of others. The community that most perfectly represents what God wants to see in the human world is one where the resources of each person are offered for every other, whether those resources are financial or spiritual or intellectual or administrative. This is the pattern of the Body of Christ as St Paul defines it. It is not only that the least or apparently most useless has the dignity of possessing a gift and a purpose; it's also that everyone is able to *give* to others, to have the dignity of being a giver, being important to someone else. And instead of being a static picture of everyone having dignity, the Christian vision is dynamic – everyone is engaged in building up everyone else's human life and dignity.

Such a vision bears very directly on the question of motivation. The religious language I have been referring to takes for granted a basic attitude of reverence, connected with thanksgiving; what is before us, the human and non-human material of the world, is mysteriously related to God and thus pregnant with God's gift for us. To interact reverently and lovingly with this human and non-human world is not only to express that basic attitude but also to open yourself hopefully to whatever gift God has for you, in whatever circumstance, or aspect of the world. It is both an unselfish approach, concerned that the human and non-human world should be not just what I want it to be but what God has designed it to be, and a self-interested one to the degree that I recognize that I cannot be what God designs me to be without the life of others also developing according to God's plan.

And the stress in Christian thinking on the active responsibility laid on each person means that whoever takes the lead, whether government or private initiative, there is a calling to be involved in the work of setting each other free to respond to the possibilities opened up by God.

The Christian vision is not therefore one in which the person's choice is overridden by a religiously backed public authority. History tells us that when churches try directly to exercise political authority they often compromise their real character as communities of free mutual giving and service; equally, when they retreat in the face of power, they risk betraying their Christian distinctiveness. Christian discipleship, it seems, means living out the vision of relationships in the Body of Christ without being afraid of conflict with the rest of society; because sometimes that living out of these relationships can be unpopular with society.

Christians, then, are not called to impose their vision on the whole of society. If they have a role in the political realm, it is that they will argue that the voice of faith should be heard clearly in the decision-making processes of society. The Christian disciple, in other words, does not campaign for political control (which would undermine their appeal to the value of personal freedom) but for public visibility – for the capacity to argue for and defend their vision in the public sphere, to try and persuade both government and individuals that a better moral basis exists for ordering public life.

How can Christians make a difference?

The greatest public influence that can be exercised by Christian disciples in a complex modern democracy is simply contained in the messages given by types of behaviour that embody the radical respect I have been talking about. Voluntary activity that conveys this message will have the potential, over time, to shift what society takes for granted. And whether or not legislation arises from this (which can only happen if an overwhelming majority of a population is persuaded of the rightness of some change – like the abolition of slavery), the climate will be different and new possibilities for human beings will be seen to open up.

The Christian hospice is a singularly powerful example of witness arising from a serious commitment to the mystery of each person made for relation with God. Another is the active involvement of congregations in monitoring their commitment to fair trade, as expressed in what they choose to buy and how they bring consumer pressure to bear on issues of production and marketing; this too can be an effective witness. In the UK, we are also developing a variety of simple ways in which individuals and congregations can monitor their environmental 'footprint' – a small but significant contribution to raising general awareness of this question as a moral and spiritual matter.

Quite often, as with the case of environmental concerns, Christian and other religious bodies are uniquely well placed to pick up those causes that have been slow to attract mainstream political support because they do not win votes. (The reform of prison conditions is another such cause that has drawn much support from churches in the UK.) It has to be recognized that the apparently rational and equitable processes of secular democracy are always vulnerable to the requirements of the electoral process – which are, sadly, not always rational and equitable.

Large-scale issues about public prosperity dominate these conflicts, and it is hard to find a hearing for other questions of longer-term significance – and longer term here does not mean less urgent. Churches and other faith groups might be called the trustees or custodians of the long-term questions, because they own a vision of human nature that does not depend on political fashions and majorities.

A healthy democracy, then, is one in which the state listens to the voices of moral vision that spring from communities that do not depend on the state itself for their integrity and meaning.

In this chapter I have been suggesting some of the specific ways in which the Christian model of humanity and the world in relation to God can open doors for renewed political vision; the Christian disciple is not seeking to make the state into a church, but is proposing to the state and to the culture in general a style and direction of common life – the life of the Body of Christ – that represents humanity at its fullest. A determinedly secular society is always in danger of becoming closed upon itself, never really coping with radical criticism, lacking a forum for discussing general moral priorities, and reluctant to change.

That is perhaps the essence of the Christian contribution in the public sphere. It is a voice that questions from a wholly different perspective, the kind of perspective that cannot be generated by corporate self-interest. It is a conversation partner, and what has sometimes been called a 'critical friend' to the state and its laws; it questions the foundations of what the state takes for granted, often challenging the shallowness of a prevailing social morality; it pushes for change to make the state a little more like the community that it is itself representing: the kingdom of God. It does not make the mistake of talking as though politics could bring the kingdom into being on earth, but it continually seeks to make the promise of the kingdom more concrete and visible in the common life of human beings, private and public.

In short, it tells the state not that it is unimportant or subordinate to some higher earthly power, just that it is relative in the perspective of God. Being disciples means being called to see others, and especially others in profound need, from the perspective of an eternal and unflinching, unalterable love. I hope and pray that we as disciples will respond to this by the strength of God's Holy Spirit, and that we can proclaim this vision as the firmest possible ground for hope in all human societies – Eastern or Western, past, present or to come.

> *Being disciples means being called to see others from the perspective of an eternal and unflinching, unalterable love*

For reflection or discussion

1 How does your Christian community act in ways that demonstrate a commitment to the dignity of every person?
2 Can you think of good examples of Christian communities, locally, nationally or internationally, making an effective contribution to public debate and decision?

6

Life in the Spirit

Live by the Spirit, I say, and do not gratify the desires
of the flesh. For what the flesh desires is opposed to the
Spirit, and what the Spirit desires is opposed to the flesh;
for these are opposed to each other, to prevent you from
doing what you want. But if you are led by the Spirit, you
are not subject to the law. Now the works of the flesh
are obvious: fornication, impurity, licentiousness, idolatry,
sorcery, enmities, strife, jealousy, anger, quarrels, dissen-
sions, factions, envy, drunkenness, carousing, and things
like these. I am warning you, as I warned you before: those
who do such things will not inherit the kingdom of
God. By contrast, the fruit of the Spirit is love, joy, peace,
patience, kindness, generosity, faithfulness, gentleness,
and self-control. (Galatians 5.16–22)

I'm going to begin this final chapter by being a bit rude
about the word 'spirituality'. It is a helpful shorthand to
talk about spirituality and spiritual life, but we ought to
be aware of just what an odd turn of phrase it is. Spirituality
is really quite a modern word. If you had asked anybody
in the fifteenth or sixteenth century, 'Tell me about your
spirituality,' they would not have had a clue what you were

talking about. 'Spirituality' for the Christian is shorthand for 'life in the Spirit', for staying alive in Christ.

First, a word of caution about supposing that there is an area of our activity called 'spiritual life' or 'spirituality'. I want to try and direct attention to the whole idea of what it means to be, and to remain, *alive in the Spirit*.

When St Paul refers to 'life in the Spirit' – as, of course, famously in Galatians 5 – what he talks about is not a set of 'spiritual' activities, but a series of very direct and simple challenges about the kind of humanity that we are living out – about *virtues*, if you like. The fruit of the spirit is love, joy, peace, patience, kindness, goodness, faithfulness, gentleness and self-control. And whenever we're tempted to think that spirituality is something a bit remote and specialized, or rather exotic and exciting, in the corner of our lives, we ought just to say to ourselves in a mantra-like way: love, joy, peace, patience . . . bog-standard human goodness. The spiritual teachers of our tradition (and other traditions too) repeatedly remind us that spiritual ecstasy is no substitute for ordinary kindness and practical generosity.

So what are we talking about in terms of 'life in the Spirit' – coming alive in Jesus Christ? I will look very briefly at four dimensions of this, and, without trying to provide a map of spiritual maturity, at least I can perhaps suggest a trail you might like to follow as you develop in your life of discipleship.

Self-knowledge

The first question that I think we ought to be asking ourselves is: 'What's keeping me human in my discipleship and my ministry?' And that leads on, instantly, to the first of my four subjects: *self-knowledge*.

To sustain yourself spiritually requires some disciplines of self-awareness. Now, that doesn't mean that you can't be a disciple without continual intense self-analysis. It's usually only in rather critical situations that we have to turn to conscious and deliberate scrutiny of our deepest motives.

> *To sustain yourself spiritually requires some disciplines of self-awareness*

But, routinely, am I capable of looking at how I'm thinking and how I'm feeling with a bit of distance, a little coolness? Am I capable of taking my intense feelings, positive and negative, out of the depths of my guts for a moment, and putting them where I can look at them – and where Christ can look at them?

It's what the ancient spiritual traditions meant by 'dispassion'. It's a terrible word, and it's not much better in Greek, because *apatheia* sounds remarkably like 'apathy', and it is indeed the source of our English word. But dispassion, *apatheia*, in the spiritual understanding of the early Christians, involved exactly that capacity to step back a fraction from how we are feeling, what we think we are wanting, and what other people are wanting. We are saying: 'Just a moment – can I make some space around these feelings, these instincts, these emotions, these desires? Can I create a bit of air around them and not allow my reactions instantly to be dictated by them?' And that applies equally to feelings of enormous ecstasy and enthusiasm as to resentment or misery. Stand back a little, give those feelings room to breathe; give yourself room to breathe. Look them in the eye and say, 'Now come on, how real are you? What's this really about?'

Self-awareness, and this rather alarming word 'dispassion', are to do with developing some sense of our freedom from the projections, the expectations, the busyness that constantly threaten to hem us in. And we only really get that when, in our prayer and in our life generally, we make enough space to hear our name spoken by God. I'm not just talking about prayer as in my talking to God, but my being still enough to hear God speaking my name, when I come to prayer saying to God, 'Tell me who I really am.'

The extraordinary resurrection story in John 21 when Mary recognizes the risen Jesus as he simply says her name, tells us a great deal about our prayer and our growth into mature discipleship. To sustain 'life in the Spirit' under pressure, we need to retain the ability to say to God, 'Tell me who I am.' Because I'm not going to settle with what everybody else is telling me – I'm not even going to settle with what *I* am telling me. I need to hear it from God, the God who tells me. Because then I know that I exist, I live, I flourish, simply because of his speaking. 'I have called you by name,' says God, 'you are mine' (Isaiah 43.1). And on that divine speaking of our name rests our whole being. Something in our prayer is about quarrying down to that level where we can hear that God is creating me and you, now in this minute – breathing our names into the world, making us alive.

Stillness

Self-awareness, then – which, as I've tried to spell out a bit, isn't just about digging around in our motivations all the time, but rather finding that freedom from the immediate noise of expectations and projections and demands, the freedom to hear my name from God – leads directly into a second area, which is *stillness*.

> To hear what God is saying we need a degree of stillness – stillness of body as well as of mind or heart

To hear what God is saying we need a degree of stillness – stillness of body as well as of mind or heart. 'Be still, and know,' says the psalmist (Psalm 46.10). Be still, and know – because I begin to know who God is, who

I am, what the world is, when what one poet called 'the storms of self' have calmed down a little bit. And I would stress that the stillness of the body is a part of this. I have often quoted the words of the seventeenth-century saint Francis de Sales given to a lady who was asking his advice about spiritual direction. He said, 'I'll start giving you spiritual direction when you have begun to walk more slowly, talk more slowly and eat more slowly.' Our stillness has a great deal to do with being aware of our behaviour in all these everyday matters. Am I giving out the impression of always being utterly driven, compelled in everything I do, in such a way that I cannot stop and listen?

Silence, it is said, is the sacrament of the age to come – a phrase from one of the great Syrian saints, Isaac of Nineveh. And if, in our prayer and our Christian life generally, we are trying to live the life of the future, the life of the kingdom, stillness is part of that. Silence of word, stillness of body. And silence of word, of course, doesn't just mean not saying anything (although that is always quite a good idea!); it can mean finding ways of saying, ways of speaking, that settle and still you: the small phrase, repeated, that doesn't break the silence. Like waves on the beach on a calm day; just the beat of a heart; small words, small phrases that keep us steady and hold us when everything else is pushing us around.

Many Christians use the 'Prayer of Jesus' for this purpose, as it has been developed in the Eastern tradition: 'Lord Jesus Christ, Son of God, have mercy on me, a sinner.' For others it can be the words of a familiar hymn, a verse of a psalm, a saying of Christ from the Gospels, or the ancient Syriac phrase quoted by St Paul: '*Maranatha*, Come, Lord.' Something we can say in order to anchor ourselves where we are.

It has sometimes been said that the real problem in prayer is not the absence of God but the absence of us. It's not that God isn't there; it's (nine times out of ten) that we are not. We are all over the place, entertaining memories, fantasies, anxieties. God is simply there in unending patience, saying to us, 'So when are you actually going to arrive? When are you going to sit and listen, to stop roaming about, and be present?'

Self-awareness and stillness are very much connected with each other, because as we still ourselves we become more likely to be able to hear God speaking our name in that mysterious moment when we connect with the act and word of God that has brought us into being and, much more important, *is* bringing us into being, moment by moment.

People are sometimes surprised, in discussion of what 'creation' means, when they are told that creation is happening *now*, because God is eternally uttering the word, the name, that is making me real, now. If God stopped uttering that word, that name, you and I and the whole universe,

> *God is eternally uttering the word, the name, that is making me real, now*

Betelgeuse and Alpha Centauri and everything at the end of millions of light years, would just stop being there. God is creating now: creation is not something that happened a long time ago, it is happening today. And somehow, in our stillness, we are seeking to connect with that moment of creation, the eternal reality of God speaking, God giving, God calling us into life.

Growth

Awareness, stillness and, third, growth: God calling us into life – 'calling', a word that suggests that there is always something ahead. Am I expecting to grow in the life of the Spirit? It's a sad reflection on any Christian if we come to the point of thinking, 'Well, I've done my spiritual growing. I've reached a point that suits me. I've found a style of discipleship that I'm comfortable with.' Yes, it's important to find a way of being, praying, speaking, singing, worshipping that you can live with; but we have to be very careful of confusing that settling down with something that won't stretch or challenge us.

We need to ask whether we come to prayer, and try to live as Christ's disciples, in the expectation of being stretched. Do I expect there to be a bit more of me at the end of a period of prayer or worship than there was at the beginning? Because that is really what it's about – whether there will be a little more of me afterwards. Or, to change the metaphor, will God have cleared away some of the clutter during that time, and created a little more space there for his life?

It is too difficult to measure; we can't look at ourselves and note down before a period of prayer or act of worship, 'This is what I am now,' then at the end observe, 'Good, now there's a little bit more.' We have to go on in the sometimes rather demanding trust that we are being pushed, pulled, enlarged, in that process, bit by bit, approaching our prayer and our discipleship with the expectation that we will be, gently, and sometimes not so gently, urged towards that new level of life.

St Paul's language in Philippians about 'stretching forward to that which is ahead' (Philippians 3.13) was a very important image for early Christians. 'Straining forward', *epektasis*, is being pulled out towards what is ahead of us. But *straining* forward is probably the wrong language, because it can suggest that it's all about me making an effort rather than God drawing me out. To expect to grow, to approach our prayer and our acts of worship with the quiet assumption that at the end of the exercise there will be slightly more of me than there was at the start, this is what we're called to do in sustaining 'life in the Spirit'.

Joy

This opens up the fourth and last of our themes for reflection, the one that is both the easiest and the hardest to talk about: *joy*. To be opened up in this way is to discover joy: not happiness, not a transient feeling of euphoria, or feeling it's basically all right in a kind of shoulder-shrugging way, but joy – the sense that we are connected with something so real that it will break every boundary or container we try to confine it in, a sense of something overflowing, pushing outwards. 'Out of the believer's heart shall flow rivers of living water,' says Jesus in the Gospel of John (7.38), about the person who receives the spirit.

Overflow, superabundance: that is what this joy is about. That is what is happening in the life of discipleship – focused as it is in the life of prayer and public worship – something boundary-breaking, something uncontainable. Joy is one of the names we give to this, because when we look at it and compare it with other experiences we know about, that is what it is most like.

One of the worst things that we as Christians can do (and have done) to the gospel is somehow to convey the impression that joy should be the very last thing on our minds, or in our hearts, in our worship or in our relation with one another. It's often as if whenever the overwhelming joyfulness of God begins to impinge on us somebody in the Church always says, 'You can't do that here.' Whether it's the exuberance of Renewal and the Charismatic Movement; whether it's the overwhelming things that literally leave us flat on our face in adoration; whether it's the moment of extreme and focused simplicity and stripped bareness when, in a whitewashed room with a plain cross on the table, we can feel that this is all there is and all that matters . . . God help us if our impulse is to say, 'You can't do that here,' or 'Let's get back into the proper channels.' Too often the message we give to the world around us is nervousness about God, rather than joy – and, of course, there is the nervousness about one another that goes with this; which is another story.

What keeps us going as disciples? Self-awareness and stillness, growth and joy. Those are the building blocks of a life of discipleship that can stand up to everything around us, in the Church and the world and in ourselves, that tries to stifle our efforts to stay spiritually healthy.

How much of ourselves are we ready to know? What helps us be still? Are we prepared to be quietly and positively willing to move on? And are we ready for the overflow, the excess of joy that can come with that? If

> *How much of ourselves are we ready to know? What helps us be still? Are we prepared to be quietly and positively willing to move on?*

we are able, somehow, to go on asking ourselves those questions, we may have no guaranteed recipe for success, but we will at least be giving God the opening to enter our lives and be at home in us. We will be offering to God our longing to be with Jesus, wherever he may lead; and in doing that we will have learned something about being disciples.

For reflection or discussion

1 Have a look at St Paul's list of the fruit of the Spirit in Galatians 5.22–23: how do you see them connecting with each other and with your own efforts to live in the company of Jesus?

2 What helps to slow you down and still your mind? How can you use this to open up a bit more space for God?